country chic

TABLE
SETTINGS

country chic

TABLE
SETTINGS

S<small>USAN</small> E. M<small>ICKEY</small>

Sterling Publishing Co., Inc.

New York

Prolific Impressions Production Staff:

Editor: Mickey Baskett
Creative Design: Susan E. Mickey
Photography: David Bjurstrom
Copy: Phyllis Mueller
Graphics: Lampe Farley Communications
Styling: William Bloodgood, Ann G. Wrightson, Susan Eldridge
Special environment assistance: Roger Foster
Administration: Jim Baskett

Library of Congress Cataloging in Publication Data
Mickey, Susan E.
    Country chic table settings / Susan E. Mickey.
        p. cm.
    Includes index.
    ISBN 0-8069-6875-3
    1. Table settings and decoration. I. Title.

TX871 .M55 2002
642'.8--dc21

2002030401

10 9 8 7 6 5 4 3 2 1

Published by Sterling Publishing Company, Inc.
387 Park Avenue South, New York, N.Y. 10016

Produced by Prolific Impressions, Inc.
160 South Candler St., Decatur, GA 30030
© 2003 by Prolific Impressions, Inc.

Distributed in Canada by Sterling Publishing
c/o Canadian Manda Group, One Atlantic Avenue, Suite 105
Toronto, Ontario, Canada M6K 3E7
Distributed in Great Britain by Chrysalis Books
64 Brewery Road, London N7 9NT, England
Distributed in Australia by Capricorn Link (Australia) Pty. Ltd.
P.O. Box 704, Windsor, NSW 2756 Australia

Printed in China
All rights reserved
Sterling ISBN 0-8069-6875-3

Acknowledgement and Humble Thanks to:
Replacements, Ltd., Greensboro, North Carolina (1-800-737-5223 or www.replacements.com)

Rachel Baba of Star Provisions, a cook's marketplace and gourmet dishware store, Atlanta, Georgia (404-365-0410), for use of the store's wonderful dishware and linens.

Anne Quatrano of Bacchanalia Restaurant, Atlanta, Georgia for allowing us to photograph in her lovely restaurant.

Thanks **to graciousstyle.com** for providing information and ideas about luxury table linens.

Contents

Introduction

GATHER 'ROUND MY TABLE AND EXPERIENCE THE COLORS and textures. Collect inspiration and ideas from these casual tables, created for friends and family at my farm and in my community. This book is intended to motivate and guide you, so your daily life and special holidays will shine with style.

As a child, I set the table every evening. (Yes, there was a time when families gathered at the table for an evening meal.) This experience began my journey of a lifetime of setting tables. I love assembling pieces of crockery and dishware and witnessing the good times of eating, laughing, and talking around a central altar filled with food. I enjoy using the chipped pieces of my grandmother's Depression glass just as much as my new French earthenware bowl, and I get great pleasure from putting them together and making the new combination sing.

I think it's important to know the proper rules about table setting—and then break them just as you please. (Like a recalcitrant youngster, sometimes I just want to put everything on one side of the plate and tie it up!) I have tried to supply simple guidelines for the "correct" way to set a table and pictures of ideas of how to offhandedly ignore those rules. Please be cavalier and suit yourself. If you are entertaining guests for whom you feel it necessary to toe the line, you'll learn to take care of that situation as well!

Finally—I have spent a lifetime collecting and admiring fine crockery, china, flatware, and crystal. Sometimes it is difficult to know what you are buying and how to care for it. I have tried to supply simple guides for choosing and collecting tablesetting elements. I endeavor to explain the difference between stainless, silverplate, and sterling; what is crockery, what is bone china, and how to know the real thing. Although my collection is not filled with Limoges and Baccarat, I like recognizing quality when I see it at a bargain price at a yard sale!

To use this book, keep it on the shelf with your cookbooks and your dictionary so these ideas can be yours every day. Thanks for coming to dinner!

— *Susan E. Mickey*

start
Simple

What's the occasion?

It doesn't take much of an excuse to want to do a little entertaining and gather folks together. It can be as simple as needing to work late with colleagues in an informal atmosphere—call it a "buffet and meeting" evening at your house. You may want to share your latest travel saga with friends or shower a couple with wedding well wishes. There is always a reason to get together and break some bread. Food, conversation, and sincere hospitality are all you need for a really successful gathering. The presentation of the meal is one more ingredient in the satisfying entertaining recipe. The setting is part of what makes people feel welcome and happy to be in your company.

Once you have decided why you want to throw a fete, stick to your purpose. You can get thrown off the track with party planning and cooking. If you just want to see your buddies on Friday night, remember why you invited them over in the first place, and don't get too caught up in a frenzy of over-preparation. Keep it simple and to the point. Sometimes you want to dress up and wear high heels, and sometimes you want to relax in flip flops. Decide which it is today and invite people to join you. You can set an impressive table without all the fuss of a state dinner.

The tablesettings in this book are examples of how you can use what you have to create great ambience. You don't have to go out and buy new and expensive dishware and linens when you want to create a special table. Look around and use what you have, or visit a flea market to discover great and inexpensive items to make your table unique. As you will see with each table, I have gathered new, used, heirloom and handmade pieces to create the themes shown. The pieces blend to make for a very creative setting.

Select a Surface

The table is the foundation of the meal service, where the people and the food come together. On Sundays at my Aunt Lucy's house, our family would sit at her kitchen table and talk for hours. Everything was discussed, diced, and hashed into a whirl of memorable conversations that formed and informed us all. I remember the smell of homemade bread and coffee, of big steaming bowls of vegetable soup and a large white linen-covered table surface with thick padding underneath to protect the wood.

At my home, we have a round rustic oak table in the kitchen with a bench and large old library chairs for long, lazy paper-reading mornings and laughter-packed, friend-filled evenings. Creating a table for receiving guests helps foster an atmosphere of welcome and hospitable cheer that encourages everyone to relax and enjoy the moment. Allow your table to speak for your individuality and proclaim your willingness to engage in the joyful pursuit of serving guests.

The surface—usually a table—is your background. It needs to be sturdy, and it needs to provide a great backdrop for the decorative elements you choose. Beautiful wood, rustic metal, vintage linens, handmade paper, even your lap—all make great surfaces for eating a meal. Consider the number of people and the type of food. Canvas your home for alternate surfaces for a unique approach—a small occasional table in front of the TV for an informal video night is a great way to get the guests and the food together. Use a bench to hold tortilla chips and dip. You can always throw pillows on the floor and eat at the coffee table.

Pick Your Plates

Your dishware determines the rest of the table elements. I like to keep a set of plain white or neutral dishes on hand—they are versatile, and you can mix and match them with many patterns and colors.

I am a shameless collector of all things dishy. I love a good yard sale, flea market, or estate sale. (The big yard sale at Replacements, Ltd. in Greensboro, North Carolina, is a dish digger's heaven—but more about that later.) Remember when you choose your dishware that mix-and-match crockery, Melmac, and paper all get the job done. You can eat with style and beauty even if you don't have the queen's china.

Grab the Glasses

Glasses are the jewels of the table that adorn the surface and allow the light to reflect and pass through. Sometimes when I set a table I frown and fuss with the whole thing, only to realize that the moment I place the stemware at each place it all comes together. I think of glassware as the crowning touch.

Find the Forks

Think through the meal and make sure you have the necessary flatware for everything you are dishing up. I have a hard and fast rule: I don't set anything that will not be used—it's my campaign to rid the world of that extraneous spoon on the right of the knife that goes unused and untouched. Remember that all utensils don't have to be present plate-side. You can bring in the dessert forks in a jar or supply a bevy of teaspoons on the side for those who want to stir their after-dinner coffee.

Table Textiles

Good linens won't let you down, and a great set of napkins will spruce up any plain jane setting. Fabrics and linens are the easiest and quickest route to pulling table elements together. (The inspiration might come from a great vintage tablecloth with eye-popping colors.) Cloth napkins are easy to find at retail stores but are also in abundance at secondhand and thrift stores in retro colors and patterns. My Vera-designed napkins (seen in "Kitchen Coffee Corner") were found at a Goodwill store for a pittance. They perk up the morning with their great 1960s colors and patterns.

Special Elements

The table isn't complete until you polish it off with extras like napkin rings, placecards, and flowers. Once you get into the habit of including these details in your table, you will include them easily and quickly. Recycle your best detail concepts from table to table so you get comfortable with the notion of completing the picture.

easy
Ways to Celebrate

You don't need a grand excuse to invite your friends over for a soiree. (Maybe you just want to show off your new placemats and a great recipe for tandoori chicken.) Set the table with a few well-placed pieces of crockery, add some fresh flowers, and it's a party. The tables in this section are versatile and could be used for different occasions and circumstances.

Table pictured:
A Very Special Birthday.
See page 15 for details.

Special Birthday

I like to pair a rustic surface with refined elements and details. For this birthday celebration, the white lacy-edged china looks picture perfect with fine linens atop a distressed surface. This sophisticated, grown-up birthday table has a subtle, soft color scheme of cashmere silver gray, white, and soft moss green.

This table is also suitable for a silver anniversary, a retirement party, or a mature bridal party.

To set this table

Surface: Primitive wooden plank board table with distressed finish (antique market)

Dishware: White eyelet charger with circle salad plate and saucer to hold favor (purchased at gourmet dishware)

Glassware: Champagne flutes, medium water glasses (purchased at gourmet dishware store)

Flatware: Stainless steel, pattern - Sambonnet Hannah (gourmet dishware store)

Linens: Irish linen tea towels (Irish import store)

Special Elements: The subtle color scheme is highlighted by the soft pink of the centerpiece flowers, cherry blossoms in a pitcher vase (gourmet dishware store). The birthday cake is presented on a white lace-edged cake stand. The bottom of the cake is decorated with the cherry blossoms from the centerpiece.

Pictured at left: Irish linen tea towels make great oversized napkins. Each place is marked with a "napkin ring" made of a cut paper strip. For placecards, I printed the names of the guests on vellum sheets using the French Script font in my computer. I cut the vellum into strips and layered them over the paper napkin rings. Each is fastened on the back with a dot of clear glue.

Pictured below: Guests feel special when they receive a party favor and have a special place at the table. The party favors here are handmade soaps covered with beautiful paper, then wrapped with 24 gauge silver jewelry wire. The topknot is finished by twisting the wire around a piece of white beach glass. All supplies were purchased at a crafts store.

Sunday Lunch

In my house when I was growing up, the Sunday noon meal (we called it "dinner") was the biggest, most formal meal of the week. My memories of these meals have more to do with the incredible food than the tables, but this table setting is a tribute to those Sundays at the

homes of my parents and of my grandmother in High Point, North Carolina. Set a table with this kind of care when you want to do something special for those you love. This table could also be for a dinner for the boss, the Easter meal, or spring brunch.

The simple color scheme of cream white and blue is accented with yellow and spring green. This toile tablecloth was made from curtains a friend was selling at her yard sale. The vintage linen table runners provide a crisp white background for the intensely colored blue and yellow plates.

To set this table

Surface: Toile fabric tablecloth, made from old curtains, with white vintage table runners (found at yard sale).

Dishware: Mixed blue and yellow Wedgwood plates (vintage),
Cobalt blue salad plate (retail store),
White butter plates with gold rims, Copeland Spode pattern (old airline dishes bought at a flea market)

Glassware: 1930s clear snuff glasses (antique market)

Flatware: Mix and match vintage silverplate (china replacement service yard sale)

Linens: Irish linen damask napkins (import store), tied with cream silk ribbon.

Special Elements: Each place is adorned with a vintage teacup planter filled with *makenoi ogon* sedum and topped with a placecard. The placecards are strips of card stock that were hand lettered.

Pictured at left: To make these perfectly sized butter pats, place the butter in the freezer for 30 minutes, then use a melon ball tool to scoop out the pats. Garnish with parsley.

Pictured above: A freeform arrangement of tulips and freesia sits in a collection of beautiful white vintage water pitchers.

Mexican Fiesta

To set this table

Surface: Primitive green wooden bench (junk pile rescue)

Dishware: Combination of blue crockery bowls (from antique market) and blue cobalt plates (from retail store)

Glassware: Green-tinted pint glasses (from import store)

Linens: Vintage Mexican tablecloth, used to drape a bench, and matching napkins (inherited)

Special Elements: Brightly painted terra cotta pots with cactus and chili peppers (make them yourself; instructions included); wooden handpainted napkin rings (retail import store)

My husband's great aunt lived in New Mexico during her later years, and we inherited this terrific tablecloth from her collection. Linens like these can be found abundantly at flea markets and antique stores. Their bright primary colors provide a whimsical and festive ambience. Chips, salsa, and a rented video are always an excuse to whip out a special piece like this that is not used every day. You don't even have to put it on a table; it can serve as a backdrop, draped over a bench or chair.

This theme could also be for a Super Bowl party, a summer barbecue, or a birthday party.

Pictured at left: Colorful drink cans become part of the decor when you put them in glasses with swizzle sticks and lime slices. Place them next to the ice bucket so your guests can serve themselves easily. The swizzle sticks, collected through the years from different places, are all of the same style. Your guests will have fun comparing the destinations printed on the sides of the sticks, which help identify whose drink is where.

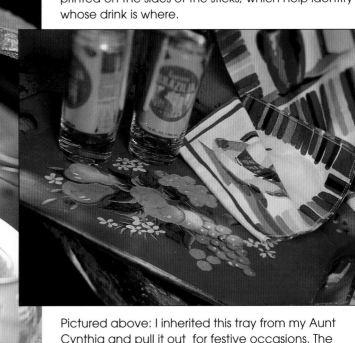

Pictured above: I inherited this tray from my Aunt Cynthia and pull it out for festive occasions. The colors continue the theme introduced by the tablecloth and napkins.

Pictured at right: Handpainted bird napkin rings have the feel of Mexican primitive folk art and accent the napkins' colorful borders.

make these
Cactus in Painted Pots

Designed By: Diane D. Flowers, MFT Enterprises

These bright, primary-colored pots are fast and easy to make, and each one is unique and different. You can swap your pots and plants by painting pots that are larger than your plant requires. Place your plant, in its original pot, inside the larger one. When you change your color scheme, remove the plant (still in its smaller pot), re-paint the larger pot, and put your plant back inside.

Supplies

Terra cotta flower pots
Acrylic craft paints - red, yellow, blue
3 paint brushes, 2"
3 paper plates
Paper towels
Optional: Outdoor sealer

Instructions

for the Large Red Pot:

1. Clean pot to be painted and allow to dry thoroughly.
2. Pour a small amount of each color of paint on individual plates, keeping the colors separate.
3. Use a paint brush to apply a thin coat of red paint over the entire pot.
4. Load a second paint brush with very little yellow paint. Holding the brush vertically, lightly rub the side of the brush against the edge of the rim and along the sides of the pot to create a dry brush effect. (The rough texture of the pot will pick up the pale yellow paint accents.)
5. Using the third brush, apply horizontal lines of blue paint randomly around the pot.
6. Finish the pot by applying a red paint randomly in spots around the pot to create variations in the deep red and lighter red colors.
7. While the paint is wet, use paper towels to blend the colors and to create color variations.
8. *Option:* Apply additional highlights using the yellow dry brush technique described in Step 4.
9. For outside use, apply an outdoor sealer.

Instructions

for the Small Green, Yellow, and Blue Pots:

1. Clean the pots to be painted and allow to dry thoroughly.
2. Pour a small amount of each color of paint on individual plates, keeping each color separate.
3. Use a paint brush to apply a thin coat of yellow paint on two pots. Use another paint brush to apply a thin coat of blue paint on the third pot.
4. Use the yellow paint brush to apply a thin coat of yellow paint randomly on the blue pot.
5. Use the blue paint brush to apply a thin coat of blue paint randomly on one of the yellow pots.
6. *Optional:* Add highlights of red, yellow, or blue by holding the desired color paint brush perpendicular to the surface and rubbing it over the sides of the pots. For added interest, create intense blocks of colors by brushing on thicker layers of paint.
7. For outside use, apply an outdoor sealer.

Painting Tip
After applying yellow and
blue paints, use paper towels
to blend the paints to create
various shades of green.

Wine Tasting

Last summer we were invited to spend two weeks at a farmhouse in Tuscany. The 17th century stone house was just outside the small town of Montalcino, and there was a gorgeous view out our kitchen window of the magical hills below. Upon our return, inspired by the wonderful food and wine of the region, we gathered friends at our house for this Italian Wine Tasting as a way of sharing our trip.

Pictured right: Each bottle is covered with two pieces of Chinese joss paper and numbered for blind tasting and evaluation. Your guests will enjoy guessing the names of the various wines, which will be revealed at the end of the evening.

Pictured left: The foods you serve can also be beautiful table details. Olives and peppers in a wooden bowl make a beautiful accent.

To set this table

Surface: Rustic plank board oak table (handmade by Roger Foster)

Dishware: Depression glass plates, Amber Patrician pattern (family heirloom on brass chargers (from import store) that have been altered with gold leafing, instructions included.

Glassware: All purpose wine glasses (retail store)

Flatware: Ivory-handled knives

Linens: Italian linen table runner with a woven pattern (souvenir of trip to Italy)

Special Elements: An antique wooden toolbox (antique market) holds bread on the sideboard; rustic iron candle holders (import store); the crock (used for rinsing and spitting) is an old family piece that helps guests feel at home.

- Announce a theme, such as "All Italian Reds," and ask each guest to bring a bottle.
- Eight is a good maximum number of wines for tasting.
- Place one all-purpose wine glass at each setting.
- A pitcher of water for rinsing and a napkin or towel for wiping the glass is a must.
- A "spit bucket" or crock is a helpful addition.

Pictured at top right: Placecards are clipped on photo holders (retail gift shop). The cards are card stock (Crane) with Michelangelo stickers (art store). On the back of the placecard is a wine rating card for guests to mark their favorites.

Pictured immediately above: Wine markers can be purchased from stores that sell beads. Adorn them with different antique buttons and beads so guests can keep track of whose glass is whose as they move about and mingle.

Pictured at left: Bread and olives are the focus of this sideboard. Candlelight adds a romantic glow.

Gold leaf Chargers and Faux Leather Balls

Designed By: Diane D. Flowers, MFT Enterprises

Simple brass chargers were brought to life with gold leaf. The reflective qualities of the brass and gold create a bright, festive contrast with the earthy hues of this table.

Gold Leafed Chargers

Supplies:

enough for eight 12" brass chargers
2 pkgs. of real gold leaf sheets
Spray adhesive for gold leaf
Sealer for gold leaf
Brown antiquing gel or stain
Soft bristle brush
Paint brush
Shallow cardboard box

Instructions for chargers:

1. Place charger in box and spray lightly with adhesive. (Putting the charger in the box helps avoid overspray on your work surface.)
2. Wait about 30 seconds for the adhesive to become tacky. Remove any dirt or adhesive from your hands and fingers. Tear sheets of gold leaf into small, irregular shapes.
3. Apply the gold leaf to the charger, using your fingers or a dry bristle brush. Press the leaf against the surface with a brush or your fingers to remove any air bubbles.
4. Repeat steps 1 through 3 until all chargers are covered. Allow to dry for one hour.
5. Use a dry soft bristle brush to remove excess gold leaf.
6. Brush a thin coat of sealer over the gold leaf. Allow to dry one hour.
7. Apply a thin coat of brown antiquing gel or stain on all of the plates. Allow to dry one hour.
8. Apply a second (thin) coat of sealer. Allow to dry 24 hours before use.

To use: Place charger under dinner plate at each place. Chargers are **not** intended for use with food.
To clean: Dust lightly with a soft, dry cloth. Do not clean with water or liquid cleansers.

Painting Tip
Use your gloved hands to hold the balls while applying paint with a paint brush. Finger marks will disappear when the final finish is dry.

Faux Leather Balls

Supplies:
one of each size

Plastic foam balls, one 6",
one 5", one 4"

4 sheets of real gold leaf

2 sheets of white tissue
paper

1/2 cup white craft glue

Small mixing bowl

Small paint brush

Liquid Adhesive for gold leaf

Sealer for gold leaf

Brown antiquing gel or stain

Acrylic craft paint - antique
white

3 small (juice size) glasses

Empty egg carton

Plastic gloves

Paper towels

2 cups water

Instructions for balls:
1. Mix water with 1/2 cup white craft glue in a small mixing bowl.
2. Tear sheets of tissue paper into irregular 4" pieces.
3. Wearing plastic gloves, attach the tissue pieces to the foam balls, using a paint brush to apply the glue and water mixture.
4. Repeat steps 2 and 3 to complete remaining balls. *Option:* For added texture, apply multiple layers of tissue.
5. Position one ball on each of the small glasses. Place the glasses on paper towels. Allow to dry 24 hours.
6. Wearing plastic gloves, paint the balls with antique white acrylic paint. Place the painted balls on the egg carton. Allow to dry one hour.
7. Using a paint brush, apply brown antiquing gel or stain. Remove excess using a paper towel. Place the antiqued balls on the egg carton. Remove gloves and clean hands and fingers. Allow balls to dry one hour.
8. Tear a gold leaf sheet into irregular shapes.
9. Randomly apply gold leaf adhesive in a small area on one ball. Use your fingers or a dry soft bristle brush to apply a piece of the gold leaf over the adhesive.
10. Continue applying adhesive and gold leaf randomly to the balls until you've used all the gold leaf. (Some areas won't be covered—that's okay. You may need to clean your hands and fingers between applications.) Place the balls on the egg carton. Allow to dry one hour.
11. Remove excess gold leaf, using a soft dry bristle brush.
12. Apply a thin coat of sealer to all balls. Allow to dry for one hour.
13. Apply a thin coat of brown antiquing gel or stain over the gold leafed areas only. Allow to dry one hour.
14. Apply a second thin coat of gold leaf sealer over the entire ball. Allow to dry one hour before handling.

Wine Ratings

	Color	Bouquet	Taste
Wine #1	❏	❏	❏
Wine #2	❏	❏	❏
Wine #3	❏	❏	❏
Wine #4	❏	❏	❏
Wine #5	❏	❏	❏
Wine #6	❏	❏	❏
Wine #7	❏	❏	❏
Wine #8	❏	❏	❏

The wine rating cards were printed on self-adhesive labels on a computer and adhered to the back of each placecard (shown on page 29). Supply pencils for easy scoring. (The fact that the pencils' color matches the mustard-and-gold color scheme is a happy coincidence.)

Afternoon Tea

The art of drinking and serving tea can be as casual or formal as you like. Brewing several pots of different teas gives your guests the option of choosing a familiar drink or tasting one they haven't tried. For this day of nibbling and sharing secrets, an old baby bed quilt serves as a tablecloth and conversation piece. If yours, like mine, was made by a family member, using it is a proud expression of family history.

A teacup collection is easy to assemble, but if you don't have enough teacups, ask each guest to bring a favorite. It's fun to see the eclectic mix and match of many different china patterns.

Fresh flowers in your chosen colors are a must. An envelope of tea bags makes a thoughtful party favor for each guest.

This table could also be a bridal shower, girlfriend's birthday, or new baby event.

To set this table

Surface: Antique baby quilt (handmade by my husband's grandmother) covering a round wooden table, topped with a square vintage white lace tablecloth (antique market)

Dishware: Small floral-motif plates, Moss Rose pattern (china replacement service) and assorted vintage teacups in the same pink floral color scheme

China Accessories: Mixed and matched teapots, creamer, and sugar bowl

Flatware: A collection of teaspoons in all shapes and sizes

Linens: Vintage pink floral linen and cotton hankies (from vintage clothing stores and flea markets)

Special Elements: Stamped placecards and teabag favors personalize each cup. A small plate under the cup and saucer can hold extra food goodies for nibbling.

Pictured left: The hankies, used as napkins, are placed in the cups with the placecards to add texture and interest. A plate for food is placed under the cup and saucer.

Pictured above: Collected over a number of years, these present a coordinated floral look though they represent a variety of patterns.

Pictured left: Ready for tea! This tea party adheres to a pastel pink and white color theme. The fresh flowers provide color accents.

Pictured right: The placecards were made with card stock, and a craft store stamp, and decorative mesh paper. I found them in a shop in Portland, Oregon called Lulu's. When I saw them, I knew they were perfect for this "gal gathering."

Pictured below: The vintage hankies used as napkins extend the pastel pink color theme and add a soft texture to the table.

making Every Day Special

Sometimes it's difficult to enjoy the small moments—times when it's just you and your family. Everyday meals can be made unique by treating yourself to the same hospitality you afford your guests. Keeping some simple, beautiful decorative elements in your cupboards helps make the routine seem rare.

Years ago I was invited to the apartment of an older woman to pick up some clothing she was donating to charity. I arrived just after she had finished her meal. Her dining room table was carefully set for one with fresh flowers, a linen placemat, a linen napkin, fine silver, and crystal stemware. The colors she had chosen were a vibrant green and shrimp. At the time, I was young and still eating on the bed in my dorm room, but I vowed to begin treating myself with that same respect.

Table Shown: Country Farmstead Breakfast. See page 38 for details.

Farmstead Breakfast

Everyone likes a hearty breakfast in the country. My grandmother made homemade biscuits nearly every day and served them with country ham. I treasure the orange juice press that sat on her kitchen counter for all of my growing-up years.

In the great Southern agrarian tradition, our family ate a big, homemade breakfast every morning. Now we reserve elaborate early feasts for certain Saturdays, but ideas from this table can make any day special, even if the menu consists of cereal or frozen waffles heated in the toaster.

Amber bakelite flatware was used for picnicking in the 1930s and 40s; it can also be found with red or green handles. The spoons are the hardest to find—I had no spoons for years. I recently saw these and snatched them up immediately!

To set this table

Surface: Round oak table (flea market)

Dishware: Floral decorated dishes, Homer Laughlin pattern (can be found at flea and antique markets

Glassware: Belgian jelly jars (antique market)

Flatware: Bakelite flatware (I got these from my grandmother, but they can be found at antique markets.)

Linens: Vintage linen napkins with yellow edging (yard sale)

Special Elements: Old crockery can be useful and beautiful as a backdrop for almost any table arrangement. The old style pitchers in the center of the table can be found at five and dime or restaurant supply stores. The familiar shapes and utilitarian nature of these pitchers make you feel right at home. Old-fashioned clothespins hold the napkins.

Syrup servers are inexpensive, attractive, and just right for honey and anything pourable—be sure to have a saucer underneath to catch any drips. Flavored syrups in a variety of servers look inviting on mornings when you're serving waffles or French toast.

Early morning food is colorful and highly decorative on its own. These cut oranges, ready for squeezing on a side table, invite participation.

Take Out

Here's an idea for times when you don't intend to cook but still want to eat in style. This meal is arranged to be eaten while sitting on pillows on the floor, but it could be served as an easy buffet. Pieces of torn-edge brown paper serve as placemats, providing a backdrop for your dishware and quick, painless cleanup.

If this meal is an extension of a business meeting, provide writing utensils for jotting down those brilliant ideas that cannot wait. (You can use the paper.) Chopsticks are a clever change of pace. Colorful Japanese origami papers make interesting coasters or bread plates.

To set this table

Surface: Slate and mahogany coffee table (handmade by Roger Foster); brown paper placemats, placed diagonally on the table, with names of guests and dish names written in red marker

Dishware: White salad plates (retail store); black noodle bowls (retail store)

Glassware: Asian beer served in bottles adds color and interest

Flatware: Red enameled chopsticks (museum gift shop or Asian grocery stores)

Linens: Asian paper napkins (museum gift shop)

Special Elements: A centerpiece of plants still in the black plastic pots from the nursery is in tune with the informality of the setting and the contemporary table. Hot towels in a black pitcher are soothing for wiping hands and faces.

Pictured above: Red, white, and black is a contemporary, elegant color scheme, and the takeout cartons become the focus rather than something to toss. I've always admired their simplicity and completeness—they look like special surprise packages at each place.
The details for this table, napkins and chopsticks, were bought at a museum gift shop. I find museum gift shops a great source for paper tableware—the things for sale there are unique, beautiful, and usually of excellent quality.

Pictured opposite page: Wet the towels and warm them in the microwave for just a few seconds. Sprinkle with a little lemon juice and serve them up for a refreshing detail. Don't forget a bowl for collecting the used towels.

Lunch

A weekday lunch need not be laborious or boring if you equip yourself with a few peppy perks. This meal is the place to showcase your clean white dinnerware and accent it with bright colors. Surround yourself with things that make you smile. A sweet note clipped to your place can make the day brighter, and even one bright flower can make a sandwich seem special.

To set this table

Surface: Stainless steel counter set with circular straw placemats (gourmet dishware store)

Dishware: Pieces from a six-piece stackable dinner set (gourmet dishware store)

Glassware: Small glass tumblers (gourmet dishware store)

Flatware: None! (We are using our fingers.)

Linens: French cotton napkins (gourmet dishware store)

Special Elements: Look to office supply stores for terrific table details. The napkin holders are metal banker's clasps; the note holder is a metal bulldog clip. I keep them in a variety of sizes and use them to clip everything from takeout menus to sandwich bags.

Pictured above: Small cups can hold dips or condiments. The napkin "ring" is a banker's clasp from an office supply store.

Pictured at right: Use parchment paper or butcher paper for chips and sandwich wraps—they make the cleanup easy and add another texture to the setting. Recycled bottles, outfitted with fabric bottle covers make snazzy vases for these bright Gerbera daisies. See the following page for how to make the bottle covers.

make a
Flower Bottle Cover

Use wool, felt, or canvas—something that is stiff and has enough body to stand up. If you use felt, you won't have to finish any raw edges. If you are making these from another fabric, cut them out with pinking shears.

Supplies for one bottle cover:
1/4 yd. fabric
Matching thread
Recycled bottle

Instructions for bottle cover:
1. Cut two bottle cover pieces from the pattern at right. (Adjust the pattern to fit your bottle by tracing it on paper and cutting at the center either horizontally (for a taller or shorter bottle) or vertically (for a wider or thinner bottle) and expanding or contracting to fit.
2. With wrong sides together, stitch side seams.
3. Press seams open.
4. Hem at top and bottom, if necessary. Trim all threads.
5. Insert bottle from the bottom of cover. If the cover won't stay standing around bottle, a piece of raffia tied around the top will do the trick.

Flower Bottle Cover pattern

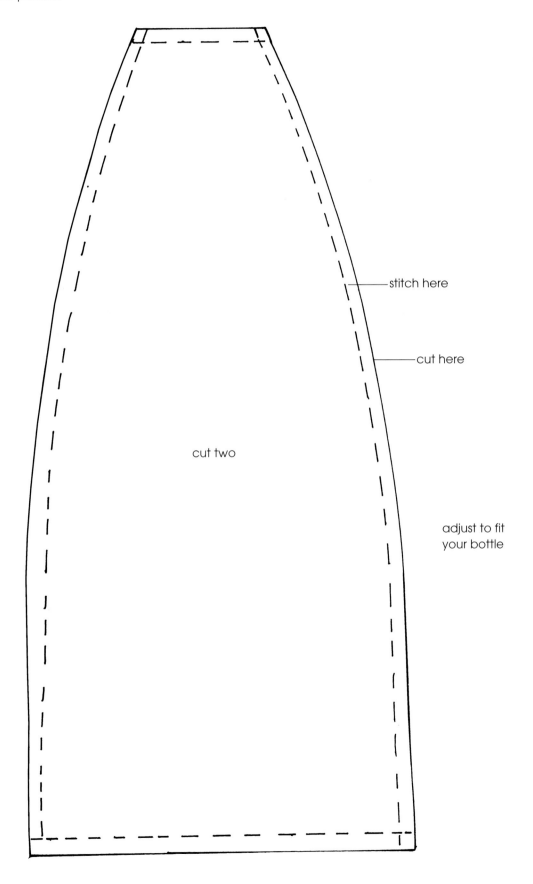

stitch here

cut here

cut two

adjust to fit
your bottle

a proper
Brekkie

Nothing is more welcome to your guest than a proper English breakfast, complete with eggs, muffins and all the trimmings. A blue and white color scheme for your breakfast table always looks fresh and is easy to highlight with one strong color. I've chosen to use orange kumquats as the centerpiece to bring in a strong color accent. The centerpiece coordinates well with the colors of the oranges and the marmalade that are being served.

To set this table

Surface: White ceramic tile table (furniture store)

Dishware: Blue and white china in Bon Marche pattern (gourmet dishware store)

Glassware: tumblers, white ceramic carafe, and syrup container, in Gio pattern. White mugs in Rosenthal pattern (gourmet dishware store)

Flatware: Stainless steel flatware in Sambonnet pattern (gourmet dishware store)

Linens: Blue linen table runners, one placed vertically, one horizontally, to form a cross; blue and white organdy napkins (all found at gourmet dishware store)

Special Elements: Kumquats on the branch are gathered in a large white pitcher..

Pictured opposite page: The folded napkin reveals the flatware. Orange scattered around the table add color and fragrance to the setting.

humble
Homestead
Holidays

Families traditionally gather at holiday times, filling your home with laughter and joy. Holidays in my family are spread out among several locations. My family comes to my house at Thanksgiving, where we eat an exceedingly large meal spread out over several hours. On Christmas night, we descend upon my close friend (also named Susan) for an informal, relaxing supper of homemade vegetable soup. Summer holidays are usually spent at my parents' lake house, where cool breezes relieve the Southern heat and we enjoy picnicking and outdoor eating during long days by the water.

Good hospitality is a gift. Your family deserves it most.

Table shown:
Thanksgiving Fall
Harvest Meal, see
page 54.

Fall Harvest Dinner

Thanksgiving Day at our farm is a food-filled, homespun affair. We serve the meal buffet or family style at one very long table or on several smaller tables positioned throughout the house. I try to take advantage of the natural gifts of the season when assembling the decorations, using dried florals and fresh nuts and berries. Warm harvest colors make everyone feel cozy and help create a table that is inviting and hearty. Copper and earthenware pottery mix happily with brown transferware for this seasonal table.

Suggest that guests—or just the kids—write "something-to-be-thankful-for" thoughts on the dried ivy leaf placecards, and ask them to share the thoughts out loud before the meal.

Pictured previous page: Handmade pottery drinking glasses are lined with squares of parchment paper and filled with dried fruits and nuts and slices of hearty bread. People can fill the mug with warm cider and munch the nibbles while they wait for dinner.

Pictured at right: You can bend the rules a bit on big holidays and tuck people in at the table a little more closely than usual. Too many people for one big table? Think of setting up smaller tables in the den or the living room. Or serve buffet style—then everyone needs only a place to perch and balance a plate.

Pictured left: For a centerpiece, arrange red pears in a low rectangular copper container and pour dried pods around them. I keep an eye out for long, low containers to use as centerpieces when I'm shopping in thrift stores and at flea markets.

To set this table

Surface: Antique pine table (antique market)

Dishware: Mix and match brown transferware (flea markets, antique markets)

Glassware: Amber fluted stemware (antique shop)

Flatware: Wood-handled stainless steel (kitchen store)

Linens: Square vintage fabric napkin over cotton jacquard placemat (kitchen store), folded together as a double napkin

Special Elements: Tuck a dried ivy leaf in each napkin as a placecard. The buffet centerpiece (page 58) is a wooden toolbox, filled with plastic pots planted with black millet. An assortment of dried pods disguises the pots (craft stores).

I like to use the real wooden surface of the table as much as possible in the harvest season. Brown transferware is enjoying a resurgence in popularity—prices vary according to a piece's collectability and quality.

Salt and pepper can arrive at the table in any number of small containers. A small vintage napkin is folded with a larger light cotton placemat to protect laps and clothes from drips and spills that inevitably come with big eating.

With the fire going and the ovens full, I use a stool by the hearth to let bread rise or warm rolls and plates.

Setting a buffet table takes planning and forethought. Using a tall focal point, like this centerpiece of black millet, makes a visually appealing display. Take a cue from professional caterers and create levels with stools or wooden boxes to place serving dishes within easy reach. Lay out your buffet a day in advance and use slips of paper to mark your dishes for what goes in what. (People laugh at me for doing this, but it works!) Try using a hollowed-out pumpkin or hollowed oranges or lemons as food containers for additional color and texture.

Brunch

This time of year, our farm is resplendent with color. Azaleas are blooming, dogwoods are flowering, and the new grass is that eye-popping shade of spring green. We serve a special brunch on Easter just after the sunrise religious services have ended.

Spring is a great time to revel in pastels. My mom found these dishes at an estate sale for a pittance, and I have continued to collect additional pieces through the years. I like to mix dishes and glassware to give the table depth and interest, and I enjoy using paper as a colorful surface under dishware. These table runners are common tissue paper embellished with cutouts—the thin paper accentuates the sunlit pastoral feeling of the morning and allows the table surface to show through.

To set this table

Surface: White painted board table (junk heap rescue)

Dishware: China in Stratford pattern (purchased at an estate sale), pink depression glass (heirloom collection), cream pitcher in Patrician Wedgwood pattern

Glassware: Pink depression glass

Flatware: Sterling silver in Madeira pattern by Towle (my Mom's wedding silver)

Linens: Yellow vintage luncheon napkins (found at a church bazaar) and wrapped in pink gingham ribbon.

Special Elements: Egg bouquets in shot glasses, tissue paper table runners, and a centerpiece of yellow eggs nesting in ribbons placed in a white china dish (see page 62). (For extra height, the dish was placed on a upside-down shallow depression glass bowl.)

Opposite page: The centerpiece is composed of dyed yellow eggs nestled in thin yellow ribbons. This is a good way to use snippets of ribbons; in this application, they are reminiscent of Easter basket grass.

These vintage yellow napkins are the smaller cocktail or luncheon size. They look like little gifts when tied with a contrasting ribbon.

Places are marked with individual egg bouquets wrapped with ribbon—the eggs are hollowed out and filled with water before adding the flowers. Each sits in an old shot glass. (Shot glasses are heavy and weighted well, so they're ideal for holding things that you don't want toppling over.) The yellow metal-rimmed tags came from an office supply store.

63

Tissue Paper Table Runners

Supplies for one four-place table:

4 pieces pink tissue paper

Scissors

Pattern

Clear glue

Instructions for table runners:

1. Fold the paper lengthwise in fourths.
2. Cut the flower pattern on the fold.
3. Unfold. Press with a warm iron.
4. When positioning on the table, a small spot of clear glue where the papers meet helps hold everything in place. 🌿

pattern for Tulip Table Runners

Cut out design on fold.

Easter Eggs

Dyeing eggs is great fun for everyone. I use food coloring, a little boiling water, and a bit of vinegar. Inexpensive wooden chopsticks make great stir sticks and double as a drying tool. To make hollowed-out eggs for bouquets, drill start a hole in the end of the egg with a drill fitted with a very small bit, then snip a slightly larger hole in that end with surgical scissors. Dump the eggs from the shells in a bowl. (Later, use them to make the pound cake.)

Butter Pats

1. Freeze a stick of butter.
2. With a sharp knife, cut butter in tablespoon-size slices.
3. Trim away corners to form leaf shapes.
4. Carve veins and details with a knife or small skewer. If butter becomes too soft as you work, refreeze and continue. 🌿

Soup Supper

A basic set of white dishes will see you through just about any occasion, and this is one element that I recommend everyone have. White dishes provide a clean palette, and they are especially effective on a brightly colored cloth or placemat, such as this Christmas place setting.

To set this table

Surface: Mahogany dining table

Dishware: White chargers and bowls (from kitchen store); red vintage fondue plates (flea market)

Glassware: Clear all purpose water/wine glasses (retail store)

Flatware: Large serving spoons used as soup spoons

Linens: Washcloths with red-stitched edges wrapped in raffia for napkins (Italian grocery store), red cotton placemats (import store)

Special Elements: The soup tureen, with red berries and greenery arranged around the bottom, is both centerpiece and serving dish.

The table is lit by small votives in vintage juice glasses on either side of the tureen.

Brass candlesticks and musical instruments decorate the periphery of the room.

Red and white linens, collected over the years, drape the backs of chairs for a note of individuality to each place.

Pictured at right: These red-rimmed glasses were a flea market find—they're perfect for serving eggnog or as votives. Oversized spoons are laid at each place for spooning the hearty soup.

Pictured below: The parting gift for each guest is a tin of homemade goodies wrapped with string and labeled with a red tag. (The tags came from an office supply store.) Have some totebags on hand for easy carrying of leftovers and takeaways.

Pictured right: These napkins are washcloths I found in Italy at a supermarket. They are very absorbent and easy for children to use. I wrapped them in raffia and included a small brass jingle bell. The red tags are an office supply store find. These red plates are vintage 1960s fondue dishes. I use them anytime I need a dash of primary color. The divisions on the plate are fun and useful for people who don't want the salad to touch the bread.

july fourth
Backyard Picnic

Make your alfresco outings easy with plastic utensils and disposable sandwich bags. The flags used here celebrate U.S. Independence Day, but you could substitute flags in a color that coordinates with what's blooming in your garden.

The blue and white enamelware was manufactured for European hospitals of another era. The red and white enamelware was a popular item in the housewares departments of variety stores in the 50s and 60s; today you can buy it at discount stores.

Pictured above: Ribs and burgers can be messy, so allow your guests the country luxury of an outdoor washroom. A pitcher of water, a basin, a towel, and a bar of soap help people clean up without tracking sand, dirt, and messy fingers into the house.

70

Pictured opposite page: Wrap sandwiches individually in white freezer paper and tie with butcher's twine. Remember to label the contents. Sandwich bags can hold food or favors—they are stamped with a star stamp (craft store) and secured with wooden clothespins.

Pictured right: This little red wagon makes transporting the whole affair a manageable ordeal. Planking placed over the top converts it to an instant buffet table.

To set this table

Surface: Rustic wooden pallets

Dishware: Red and white enamelware plates (variety, discount stores), blue and white enamelware (flea market)

Glassware: Clear canning jars

Flatware: Red plastic utensils

Linens: Rolled up blue and white men's handkerchiefs with utensils inside

Special Elements: Have a wash basin for cleaning up before, during, and after the meal. A red wagon easily carries the picnic accoutrements. White paper sandwich bags are stamped with red stars and clipped with clothespins.

Pictured above: Roll folded napkins around red plastic flatware and secure with string. For each string "napkin ring," cut a 12" piece of string. Leave a 3" tail, then wrap the string around the folded and rolled napkin. Tie a single knot to secure the napkin, trim the end of the string to match the 3" tail, and tie a double knot. (This gives you a convenient hook for carrying your napkin and utensils.)

rustic
Outdoor Gatherings

Ah, the great outdoors! I love entertaining al fresco because I don't have to vacuum before the guests arrive. Outdoor gatherings are particularly casual and help us revel in the beauty of nature.

When setting a table outside, consider the weather. If showers are forecast, have you planned an alternate location? Will your guests need protection from wind, hot sun, or insects? If the meal is to be served in the middle of the day, will guests need sun hats or umbrellas for shade? I keep a pot of hand fans by my porch door for stirring a breeze on particularly hot afternoons.

Think about how the light and temperature will change when the sun sets, and be prepared to light candles or bring out lanterns. And if it turns a little chilly, you can wrap up in a blanket and still enjoy an outdoor meal.

Table shown: Patio Barbecue. See page 76 for details.

patio
barbecue

This outdoor barbecue buffet encourages people to skewer their own food and head for the grill. The food and fruit help determine the color scheme. Use the pineapple as a centerpiece, then slice it up for dessert.

To set this table

Surface: Copper metal table (outdoor furniture store)

Dishware: Oval platters in Sprout pattern (gourmet dishware store)

Glassware: Gold tumblers(gourmet dishware store)

Flatware: Skewers and forks wrapped in napkins

Linens: Yellow striped cotton napkins (gourmet dishware store)

Special Elements: The colored Venetian champagne glass that holds the skewers is an extravagance outdoors, but it catches the light like nothing else.

Pictured at right: Tie green raffia (craft store) and a green tag (office supply store) to each glass for easy identification.

a gathering of
Gardeners

A garden party almost decorates itself. These lovely floral dishes are enhanced by the contrast of a rustic surface. The centerpiece celebrates the flowers of the season. Each place is made special (and colorful) with the addition of an apron draped and tied around the back of the chair, a favor of flower seeds and brightly colored gardening gloves, and a garden theme placecard—guests' names are written on slips of paper that resemble plant markers and tucked into glasses. The floral motifs of the seed packets, aprons, gloves, and china combine to create a gardeners' garden party.

To set this table

Surface: Rustic wood and rush table

Dishware: Violet-patterned china (a lifetime's collection)

Glassware: Etched crystal stemware (a wedding gift)

Flatware: Sterling silver

Linens: Vintage hankies, all with purple floral motifs (a collection)

Special Elements: Seed packet and garden glove favors, centerpiece of pansies and camellias, aprons in purple floral fabrics on the backs of chairs, place labels of purple paper strips with names written vertically, like plant markers.

Here's how to fold the hankies:

1. Lay out hankie diagonally.

2. Fold top corner down three-quarters of the way toward the bottom corner.

3. Flip over.

4. Fold left side just past center of hankie.

5. Fold right side just past center of hankie.

6. Flip over to reveal diagonal pocket. In the pocket of each, include a pair of cotton gardening gloves and a seed packet.

81

Leaf Peeper Picnic

Perfect picnics often require more planning than indoor meals, but the memories are worth the trouble. In the fall, I like to invite friends to ramble in the woods to gaze at the turning foliage and enjoy a picnic lunch. I provide a picnic basket (with a cloth and a blanket) and let them serve themselves at an outdoor buffet.

The colors of the changing leaves inspire this richly colored palette. Granny Smith apples and a bouquet of dried herbs and weeds decorate the serving table. Prepared salads and pickled veggies are spooned into antique blue glass canning jars. The screw-top lids keep the contents safe from ants, flies, and other uninvited guests.

To set this table

Surface: Unfinished low outdoor table

Dishware: Blue glass canning jars (flea markets), old tin plates (flea market)

Glassware: Assorted yellow crockery mugs (retail store)

Flatware: Stainless steel (retail store)

Linens: Vintage linen tablecloth with fall leaf print (vintage linen store), yellow and brown cotton napkins (kitchen store)

Special Elements: Baskets are packed with picnic gear and are ready to go. Make cards with leaf shapes for identifying foliage.

Pictured right: Natural
wax paper lines rustic
tinware plates.

Pictured right: Any deep basket can serve
as a picnic basket. Provide blankets for
sitting and tablecloths for the picnic.

Pictured opposite page: Blue canning jars
are filled with a tempting assortment of
side dishes (bean salads, potato salad,
pickled vegetables). They're easy to carry
in a basket (no spills!) and serving is simple
(right from the jar).

a refreshing
Beverage

Sometimes entertaining just means making sure everyone has something to drink. When preparing and serving a full meal seems daunting, inviting people over for coffee, cocktails, or a glass of lemonade can be more easily achieved.

I set up a "beverage station" in my home whenever I entertain a crowd—it is practical and easy for guests and keeps the wet and messy pouring and mixing in one place. It's good to supply a towel or cloth at the site for quick cleanup of spills. Locating near a water source is helpful; if that's not possible, supply a pitcher of water.

To help you plan for various types of occasions, I've supplied checklists for easy assemblage.

Pictured at right: You can pack a portable sun tea break in a primitive wooden crate. Fill it with a jar of tea, ice-filled glasses, and sliced citrus. Add napkins and a picnic tablecloth and carry it to the garden to provide a refreshing break from gardening chores. The vintage glasses are a summer staple at my house. They hold a full 18 ounces and a lot of ice. You can sip all afternoon from one glass.

Coffee Corner

The smell of fresh coffee brewing in the morning—there's nothing like it! You could keep this coffee station set up year-round or assemble it when overnight guests will be grazing all morning. Thanks to the burgeoning interest in everything coffee, you can easily find ingredients to satisfy everyone's flavor and topping tastes. It is fun to have a coffee bar at home so the long, leisurely activity of sipping and sitting can start in your pajamas.

When Serving Coffee

- Grind only enough coffee for the pot you are brewing.
- Store hot coffee in a vacuum sealed carafe. Don't reheat or boil.

Things for a Coffee Bar

Regular coffee
Decaffeinated coffee
Half and half (Keep the pitcher in a little bowl of ice.)
Lowfat milk (Ditto.)
Sugar
Sugar substitute
Cinnamon sticks
Ground cinnamon
Ground or shaved chocolate
Whipped cream
Spoons (Dip the bowl of the spoon in melted chocolate and freeze on a sheet of wax paper for a sweet treat for stirring.)
Tea towel or dish towel
Napkins

Lemonade Break

Lemons, sugar, and water—what could be more simple? Or more refreshing on a hot summer day? For this casual service, I've combined various pieces of green glass and small clear milk jugs for serving up the lemonade. Be sure to provide straws for sipping. The vintage tablecloth with yellow roses and green leaves looks wonderful with the green pressed glass.

Even if you make your lemonade from frozen concentrate, consider serving it up with green glass and yellow lemons.

Refreshing Ideas

Things to freeze into ice cubes for a cool drink:

Tiny violets

Mint leaves

Lemon or lime slices

Seasonal berries

Other beverage ideas

Flavored tea with fruit

Orange juice with fizzy water

Iced coffee (with frozen coffee ice cubes)

the
Cocktail Hour

Complete Bar Checklist

Supplies:
Bottle opener
Cocktail picks or toothpicks
Corkscrew
Cutting board
Electric blender (optional)
Ice bucket
Juice squeezer
Large glass for mixing
Long-handled spoons
Measuring cups
Napkins and coasters
Shaker
Sharp knife
Short, thin cocktail straws
Shot glasses
Strainer
Swizzle sticks
Tongs

Liquor for the well-stocked bar includes:
Amaretto
Bitters
Blended whiskey
Bourbon
Campari
Cognac
Cointreau
Gin
Kahlua
Port
Rum
Sambucca
Scotch
Tequila
Vermouth
Vodka
Wines, red and white

Inviting people over for cocktails is a way to entertain friends and colleagues for an hour or two, before they disperse for the rest of the evening. Cocktails can be incredibly elaborate or simply casual. Having a small cocktail bar set up in a corner of the dining room is convenient and festive.

I have always associated the cocktail hour with the 1950s, but thanks to its renewed popularity in the 1990s, there are retro cocktail items galore in kitchen boutiques and gift shops.

Pictured above: A collection of swizzle sticks or colorful cocktail napkins can spice up the hour.

Champagne Toast

This beautiful collection of champagne flutes has been assembled over many years and represents many years of careful choosing. Most are gifts from a dear friend and colleague, who every Christmas presents a different and unusual glass to toast the new year.

Serving Champagne

- Store your champagne in a cool dry dark place with the bottle laying on its side.
- Chill champagne in a bucket half full of ice for half an hour before serving. Champagne should be served at a temperature of between 43 and 48 degrees Fahrenheit. Never chill the glasses.
- Pour each glass two-thirds full. One bottle fills six flutes. A magnum fills twelve flutes.
- A champagne flute-style glass promotes the slow release of the bubbles. Open glasses let the bubbles escape too quickly, so the champagne becomes flat too soon.

To uncork champagne:

1. Wrap a towel around the bottle and dry off any water or condensation.
2. Tilt bottle away from you (and anyone or anything that could be hit by a shooting cork) and remove the wire cage and the foil.
3. Grip the cork in one hand with the thumb firly on top of cork. Hold the base of the bottle firmly in your other hand, with your thumb in the indentation in the bottom of the bottle and your fingers spread out around the barrel of the bottle.
4. Twist the bottle, **not the cork.** The cork should gently ease out with a whooshing sound, not a pop. (Popping releases too many bubbles.)

pretty
Pieces of

This is the reference part of the book. I've included information I wished I'd known when I started collecting and using dishware, glassware, flatware, and linens—things like how to identify fine china, how to remove a stain from a napkin, where to find more of a particular china pattern.

Information

a guide to
Table Textiles

The generic term "table linen" refers to almost anything that is made of cloth and used in the kitchen, bath, dining room, or bedroom. Specifically, linen is anything made from flax fiber.

Linens have been part of civilization from the earliest periods of recorded history. Making cloth was a domestic art and handcraft. For centuries, every home had a loom, and the household linens woven on it were cherished and prized possessions. After the Industrial Revolution, linens were machine made and readily available, but fine linens of all kinds are still family heirlooms.

What's in a name?

Some call it a "napkin." Others say "serviette" or "bib."

Embroidery

Napkins are most often embroidered (usually monogrammed) in one corner. Tablecloths can be embroidered in all four corners or in the center. White is the traditional color for embroidery. A contrasting color may be used to coordinate a particular piece of china or color scheme.

Single-letter monograms usually showcase the first letter of a family's last name. Three-letter monograms expand the possibilities; today, you can make your own rules. (Remember you want to be able to live with it forever.) If you are reticent to commit to an initial, consider a family crest or emblem that will make your linens beautiful and unique. Other suggestions are perhaps embroidered grapes for wine tastings, flowers for springtime, or dates of special occasions and banner events.

Alternative napkin ideas

Linen kitchen towels
Small terrycloth hand towels
Vintage hankies
Washcloths

Alternative tablecloth ideas

Old quilts
Old bedspreads (especially as picnic cloths)
Handwoven cotton rugs (great for hot dishes because they're thick)
Colorful shawls or scarves

For a formal dinner

Historically, "formal" has meant a lace tablecloth for breakfast and lunch and a damask cloth for an evening dinner. Of course, feel free to break the rules—but before you break them, it's nice to know what they are.

To set a formal dinner table, use padding or felt under the damask tablecloth to smooth the cloth and protect the table. Fold the dinner napkin in a basic rectangle and place it in the center of each plate. Position the placecard on top of the napkin in the center of the plate.

A formal dinner napkin is large enough to cover the entire lap when folded in half. Folding helps prevent it from sliding to the floor (oops!) and keeps spills from soaking through and soiling your clothes. Always unfold your napkin in one smooth movement (flourishes are unnecessary).

Vintage linens

They are fun to shop for and a joy to use. They are often colorful, and the prints can be inspiring.

Stack them on shelves.

Hang them over rods.

Roll them up and display them in a basket.

Vintage linens can be found on the Internet at popular e-auction sites. Also look for fine table linens at flea markets, vintage clothing stores, antiques stores, and estate and yard sales.

101

Know the fiber content

The best table linens are made of natural fibers. Tablecloths and napkins made of synthetic fibers are less absorbent and more difficult to clean. (They can really grab onto grease!) Read the labels to determine the fiber content. Keep shopping until you find linen, cotton, or flax. (Silk can provide an elegant underlayer for a formal occasion, but most silk items must be dry cleaned.)

TYPE	DESCRIPTION	QUALITY
Damask	Fabric with a woven pattern. Originally of silk, the fabric was richly woven into textures and patterns of fruit, flowers, animals, and ornaments. Around the 12th century artisans in the city of Damascus, long known for the quality of their weaving, began to loom designs that surpassed all others for fineness and beauty, and the traders of the day began calling every richly designed and curiously woven fabric "damask." Today we call almost any tablecloth with a woven pattern a damask tablecloth. They can be made of cotton, linen, or a blend.	In cotton or linen, a damask napkin or tablecloth is an excellent choice.
Lace	Lace cloths are usually made of cotton that is woven, knitted, crocheted, or tatted in intricate, open designs. Lace cloths can appear in a large variety of patterns. Very fine lace may be of Venetian, Irish, or Dutch origin.	The fineness of the thread and the intricacy of the pattern determine the quality.
Linen	Cloth made from flax fiber. Most vintage table linens and more costly table coverings sold today are made of linen. Fine linen is often from Ireland or Belgium, but I have seen exquisite quality in French and Italian linens.	Excellent quality; always a welcome addition to a well-set table.
Handkerchief Linen	An extremely lightweight linen, originally designated for (what else?) handkerchiefs. Finely and tightly woven, handkerchief linen cloths have a high thread count.	Excellent quality.
Cotton	Any cloth made of cotton fiber. Cotton linens are common today; they are what you find for sale in major retail stores.	Best quality cottons are labeled "Egyptian" or "Pima."
Paper	A great disposable option, whether handmade paper, crinkled paper, old maps, lace paper doilies, brown kraft paper—even newspaper—for tablecloths. Paper napkins are available in a variety of lively prints and a huge range of solid colors.	Quality matters most for napkins—the heavier and softer the paper, the higher the quality. (You can feel it when you wipe your mouth!)
Woven Grass or Tatami	Any woven mat or cloth of fibrous natural straw or grasses.	The finer the weave, the higher the quality. Examine mats for loose ends or straggling fibers.
Laminated	Any mat or table covering (cloth or paper) with a plastic coating or finish; some are hard finish plastics.	Laminated cloth is preferable, although there are attractive plastic alternatives.

DURABILITY	POPULAR USES	+/-
Fairly durable; however, the intricate jacquard weave can show wear. Avoid coarse scrubbing or rubbing for stain removal, as threads tend to separate.	Considered more formal, usually used for special dinners. An excellent wedding gift or heirloom.	+ Always sets a beautiful, elegant table. -/+ Not as long lasting as other linen or cotton weaves, but well worth the expense if formality is desired.
Durable **only** when cared for properly. Hand washing is a must to prevent ripping and pulling of delicate threads.	Lace cloths have a particularly feminine, old-fashioned feel. They are highly appropriate for special occasions celebrated among women. In a formal household, they were used for breakfast or lunch.	- Lace is more work to clean and store. + Supplies a beautiful contrast in texture when placed on a solid-colored cloth or directly on a wooden table. The fact that you can see through lace presents the opportunity for layering.
Flax is a slightly heavier material than cotton but its dry strength is about double that of cotton. Because of multitude of the structure and length of flax fibers, linen cloth can be smooth and lustrous.	Multitudes	+ Any occasion is appropriate for a good linen napkin or tablecloth—it's universally accepted. + It does not stain as easily nor absorb or hold moisture as liberally as cotton. -/+ It can be costly, but is a good investment and a lasting heirloom.
Not as durable because of the extremely fine fibers.	Luncheons and formal breakfasts—any meal that requires a lighter, daintier setting.	- Slightly fragile. + Lasts when cared for properly.
Cotton is very durable, strong, and absorbent. Cotton items grow softer with use.	Most casual and informal daily meals are appropriate for good cotton napkins, placemats, and tablecloths.	-/+ Cotton will shrink more than linen but can be machine-washed with ease.
Higher quality napkins are heavier and more durable. If you are serving messy food like barbecue, get heavy napkins!	Any casual, outdoor, or large gathering.	+ Disposable (Environmentally speaking, recycled paper products are an excellent choice.) + Generally inexpensive.
Highly durable if stored flat or rolled.	Great for casual entertaining and outdoor eating and serving. Woven straw insulates and protects tabletops.	+ Adds a rustic, textured element to a table that is achieved in no other way. + Are best cleaned by wiping with a damp cloth. - Not easily cleaned of serious food spills.
They last (and last, and last).	Great on casual tables; a must when entertaining small children.	+ A way to make a kid's table more fun—laminate your own or buy them. + Easily cleaned and reused.

103

care
for your Linens

The key to keeping linens stain-free is getting them clean as quickly as possible (without whipping the tablecloth out from under still-grazing guests, of course!) Treat food or beverage stains according to the chart below.

Put **machine washable linens** to soak in the washing machine. After soaking, wash as directed and dry on low heat in the dryer or line dry. Store when completely dry.

Wash **vintage and delicate linens** by hand in a washtub. You can buy special washing compounds for linens or simply use non-chlorine mild bleach and detergent for your white pieces. After washing, lay them flat on a towel and roll the towel to squeeze out excess water. Lay them flat to dry or hang in the sun to continue the bleaching process.

General care tips

- Always test a small hidden section of fabric before applying a detergent or solvent to the surface.
- Never wash colors with whites.
- Wash in warm water and tumble dry on medium to light heat.
- Always pre-treat stains.
- Store napkins flat or folded in fourths.
- Hang tablecloths on large coat hangers.

Supplies for quick and easy stain removal

Ammonia
Baking soda
Club soda
Cornstarch
Detergent
Drycleaning solvent
Enzyme presoak stain
  remover
Household salt
Hydrogen peroxide
Lemon juice
Rubbing alcohol
Talcum powder
White vinegar

STAIN	PRE-TREATMENT	WASH
Candle Wax	Chill with ice, scrape off as much as possible. Iron wax stain between two layers of paper towels. Change towels as they absorb the wax.	Launder in warm, soapy water.
Catsup or Tomato Sauce	Soak for 10 minutes in cool water. Sponge with liquid dish detergent. Rinse thoroughly.	Launder in warm, soapy water.
Chocolate	Rinse for 10 minutes in cool water. Apply an enzyme pre-soak stain remover. Let sit 30 minutes. Rinse thoroughly.	Launder in warm, soapy water.
Coffee or Tea	Sponge immediately with cool water. Stretch over a bowl and pour boiling water from high above the fabric. Blot with a vinegar-soaked cloth. Rinse thoroughly.	Launder in warm, soapy water.
Fruit or Berries	**Caution:** Soap will set stain. **Do not apply soap.** Rinse with cool water. Soak for 30 minutes in enzyme pre-wash stain remover. (For old stains, sponge with white vinegar.) Rinse thoroughly.	Launder in cold water. If stain persists, launder in a light solution of chlorine bleach and water.
Gravy	Soak in baking soda and cold water for 15 minutes. Sponge with white vinegar and soak in cold water with mild detergent for 30 minutes. If stain persists, use an enzyme pre-wash stain remover. Rinse thoroughly.	Launder in warm, soapy water.
Lipstick	Blot with drycleaning solvent, holding a paper towel or other absorbent disposable material behind the stain. Continue until color is removed. Rinse thoroughly. Sponge with liquid dish detergent until stain is gone. Rinse thoroughly.	Launder in warm, soapy water.
Mustard	Work liquid dish detergent and a few drops of vinegar into the stain. Rinse thoroughly. If stain remains, apply a 3% solution of hydrogen peroxide. Rinse thoroughly.	Launder in warm, soapy water.
Red Wine	**Caution:** Soap will set stain. **Do not apply soap.** Sprinkle stain generously with table salt. Let salt absorb the stain. Sponge with cool water and club soda. Rinse thoroughly.	Launder in warm, soapy water.
Soft Drinks	Soak in warm water, detergent, and a few drops of white vinegar for 30 minutes. Rinse thoroughly.	Launder in warm, soapy water.
Rust	Treat area with lemon juice and salt. **Do not** use chlorine bleach—it will set the stain. Or use a commercial rust remover, following manufacturer's instructions. Rinse thoroughly.	Wash in warm water with mild detergent.

does size matter?

A standard napkin is 18" to 22" square. Formal specifications call for a 26" square napkin. (Today, that could double as a skirt!) Cocktail napkins are usually about 11" square.

A tablecloth has a standard drop (the part that hangs off the side of the table) of 8" to 12" per side, but if you use fabric pieces or alternative toppers, let your eye be your guide. For an elegant table, I love a drop all the way to the floor. Most manufactured tablecloths come in standard sizes. The measurements reflect the standard drop.

If your table measures:	Your table will seat:	If your table shape is:	Your tablecloth size is:
28" x 28" to 40" x 40" square	4	■	52" x 52" square
36" diameter to 48" diameter round	4	●	60" round
28" x 46" to 40" x 58" oblong	4 to 6	▬	52" x 70" oblong
28" x 45" to 40" x 58" oval	4 to 6	⬭	52" x 70" oval
46" to 58" diameter round	8	●	70" round
36" x 60" to 48" x 72" oblong	6 to 8	▬	60" x 84" oblong
36" x 58" to 48" x 70" oval	6 to 8	⬭	60" x 84" oval
64" to 76" diameter round	6 to 8	●	90" round
36" x 78" to 48" x 90" oblong	8 to 10	▬	60" x 102" oblong
36" x 78" to 48" x 90" oval	8 to 10	⬭	60"x 102" oval
36" x 96" to 48" x 108" oblong	12 to 14	▬	60" x 120" oblong
36" x 96" to 48" x 108" oval	12 to 14	⬭	60" x 120" oval

Quality Details

- Excellent construction
- Fine workmanship
- Finely woven natural fiber fabrics—smooth, soft, and lustrous, but never shiny; no coarse knots or slubs.
- Napkins with a full hem (at least 1"), mitered corners (a sign of good quality), or a hem-stitched edge (they will last, not ravel away).

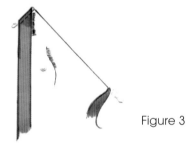

Figure 1

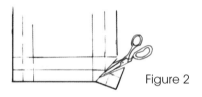

Figure 2

Figure 3

Figure 4

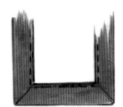

Figure 5

make a
Simple Napkin

Supplies for four 18" napkins:

Scissors
1-1/4 yards fabric, 45" wide
Matching thread
Scissors

Step-by-step:

1. Wash and dry fabric. Press flat.
2. Cut four 22" squares of fabric.
3. On all four sides, fold down a 1" hem of fabric to wrong side. Press. (Fig. 1)
4. Fold under 1" again. Press.
5. Unfold fabric and trim across each corner sto make a nice miter. (Fig. 2.)
6. Fold down the first 1" hem to wrong side and stitch down.
7. At corners of napkin, place the right sides of the hem together and stitch across corners, at an angle to edge of fabric. (Fig. 3.) Trim off extra fabric at corner triangles. Press seams open. (Fig. 4)
8. Turn the second hem under 1", turning under on wrong side of fabric. Press.
9. Stitch hem on machine next to folded edge of fabric, or hem by hand using an overhand stitch. (Fig. 4). Press flat.

make a
Tablecloth

Measure the table. Determine the size of the cloth by adding the drop plus 2-1/2" to each dimension, then figure how much fabric you'll need. Be sure to allow for shrinkage. Wash and dry fabric. Cut out. Press and stitch, following the instructions for making a simple napkin, but increase the hem to 2-1/2".

Pictured below: This table was set at a beach house at Martha's Vineyard using a sarong-type swimsuit coverup as a tablecloth.

the dish on
Dishes

Even if you're serving finger foods, you still need something to put them on. Not surprisingly, plates and vessels are among the earliest known man-made objects—archaeologists have found that even the most primitive peoples used objects to store, carry, and serve food and water. Because some of the earliest dishware was crafted and decorated by the Chinese, we generically refer to all table ceramics as "china."

choosing your china

So much china, so little time. It is hard to choose one kind to live with for your whole, entire life. In fact, it's downright impossible! So start out by choosing something to eat dinner on, and then work up to the rest. China is like fine wine—if you like it, it is good—your taste is all that really matters. Selecting the first piece is the hardest, so I have devised a guide to get you going. Keep in mind that it is better to have bad taste than no taste at all, and jump in and start digging for dishes.

Considerations

Weight

How heavy do you want your plates to feel in your hand? Do you like a substantial piece of crockery or fine, thin, translucent bone china? (There is no wrong choice.)

Ease of cleaning/ heating

Decide whether table-to-microwave is important. If it is, make that consideration part of your decision.

Availability

Is it more important to have a matched service for 24 or one really good dish you like a lot? Does mix-and-match work for you? A good department store or kitchen shop can help you assemble complete sets of matched or companion patterns, so you won't have to search the china tables at flea markets. (I personally think that it is one of life's great pleasures—but to each her own!)p

DISHWARE	DESCRIPTION	QUALITY
Pottery	Made of clay, fired at lower temperatures. Usually somewhat porous. Thickish in appearance and heavy in weight. A country or casual choice.	Highly variable, depending on the maker. Check for lead content before using.
Earthenware	Looks similar to pottery. Lightly fired to the point of vitrification. Readily absorbs water unless glazed. Opaque and dense. Suitable for everyday use.	Good. Check for lead content and to see if dishwasher safe.
Stoneware	Clay that is fired at a very high temperature, making it hard, dense, and opaque. Water resistant.	Good quality.
Porcelain	Soft paste: Made from a paste of white clay and ground glass; fired at an extremely high temperature. Hard Paste: Made from china stone and kaolin; fired at a higher temperature than soft paste. Both are nonporous and translucent.	High quality.
Bone China	Refined clay and bone ash fired at very high temperatures.	Excellent quality. Lighter weight than porcelain and whiter in color.
Tinware	Enamel-coated tin. Transfers heat from hot food.	Basic.
All-Purpose	Includes anything that can go from the microwave to oven to dishwasher to table to the fridge.	Excellent quality for its purpose.
Woodware	All bowls and plates made from tree products and plants such as bamboo. Must have special finish for food use.	Good basic quality for serving pieces, chargers, or salads.
Paper	Anything made of paper for food use.	Quality varies with thickness and finish.

DURABILITY	POPULAR PATTERNS	+/-
Chips easily. Not always dishwasher safe. Must be stacked carefully. Not recommended for daily use.	Pottery may be hand thrown by an artist or manufactured (e.g., Pfaltzgraff or Stangl)	+ Can add beautiful texture and individuality to a table. - Requires more care.
More durable than pottery. Generally dishwasher safe.	Fiestaware by Homer Laughlin, Desert Rose and Apple by Franciscan, creamware, majolica, and delft.	+ Colorful, fun patterns of earthenware can set a pretty table. + Can be fun to collect. - May need special care. + Great for informal entertaining.
Very durable. Usually dishwasher and oven safe; sometimes microwave safe. Great for every day.	Some of the most popular are Mikasa and International.	+ Affordable, easy to find, easy to use. + Especially good for everyday use and entertaining large numbers. + Excellent informal choice.
Hard paste is more chip-resistant than soft paste. Because of the fine nature, it is sometimes fragile. Handled with care, it will last.	Blue Garland by John Haviland, Holiday and Weatherly by Lenox.	+ Excellent for formal entertaining. - Though less expensive than bone china, can still be quite an investment. - Requires ample storage for proper stacking and care. + Many patterns to choose from; readily available.
Less brittle than porcelain. Lasts if handled carefully.	Old Country Roses by Royal Albert, Pembroke and Gold Trim by Aynsley, Charnwood and Florentine by Wedgwood.	+ Excellent for formal entertaining and special occasions. - Expensive + Can be a good investment; usually considered a family heirloom to be passed down and cherished. - Difficult to store, as it needs proper padding and space.
It's metal and doesn't break. Will chip if used too forcefully, but lasts forever if handled properly.	N/A	+ Great for picnics. + Can be affordably collected and easily stored. + Good for households with children and pets.
Will last forever (unless you throw it against a brick wall).	Corel, CorningWare, Fire King, Pyrex	+ Affordable and easy to use. + Available at major discount stores. + Great for kids and everyday use. - (Sometimes) very little visual value.
Great longevity with proper care.	Most major houseware stores, crafts galleries.	+ Can add a texture and depth to a table setting. + Good for outdoor summer events. - Not suited for anything hot or wet; should not be left in water. - Needs to be oiled with an edible oil (such as salad oil) occasionally.
Entirely disposable.	Best ones found at museum gift shops and specialty party stores.	+ Great for outdoor picnics, informal gatherings with large numbers. + Choose high quality to avoid accidents and spills. + Recycled products available.

Digging for Dishes

There is a very special place for those of us addicted to collecting china, flatware, glassware, and all things for the table. I was told about this magical kingdom by my sister. "If you need to replace some china, call them," she said nonchalantly.

I found Replacements, Ltd. on the Internet and was intrigued. The company's specialty is identifying and locating china patterns. You send a picture or a detailed description, and they identify it and put you on the mailing list for pieces as they receive them. Bob Page started this business to satisfy his lifetime interest in antique and used tableware. He began by going to yard sales and estate sales and picking up pieces for friends and acquaintances with a record keeping system on 3 x 5 cards.

It was not until I visited the company facility in Greensboro, North Carolina that I realized what a lot of china in one place can do for your heart. Replacements has an annual "yard sale" to clear out its warehouse. They drag out boxes and boxes just filled with discontinued, damaged, and discarded goods. The boxes are lined up, row after row, on a sweeping field in the open air. For a dish digger like me, it's a little like the Olympics.

I traveled there with my mother, my friend Carol, and my sister-in-law. We found dishes for ourselves, dishes for our families, dishes for our friends, and dishes we never realized we needed. We stooped and picked and examined more china in one day than I ever thought was possible, while my father waited patiently on the sidelines and dutifully manned the filled-and-waiting-to-be-purchased boxes we brought him.

The good people at Replacements—a staff of 700 people—sort, clean, and evaluate dishes every day (indoors, of course). The warehouse is the size of four-and-a-half football fields, and the showroom covers 12,000 square feet. A museum at the company headquarters houses 2,000 rare pieces of china, crystal, and silver, plus collectible plates and figurines. Now in its twentieth year, the company serves four million customers from around the world, and annual sales are an amazing $71 million.

Proper dish cleaning

Check with the manufacturer before putting plates in the dishwasher. If in doubt, don't. Plates with metallic trim should **never** go in the dishwasher.

In the dishwasher:

- When loading, place dishes so that they do not touch each other.
- Do not use a high heat setting—this may damage fine china. Use the gentle cycle (sometimes labeled "china") and air dry without heat.
- Allow china to cool to room temperature before removing and storing.

By hand:

- Remove all jewelry (bracelets, watches, rings) before washing dishes.
- Use a mild liquid soap.
- Place a rubber mat or tub insert in the sink to prevent chips. Attach a rubber nozzle to your faucet.
- Sort dishes before washing (glassware first, spoons and forks next, then plates, then serving dishes, cooking utensils, and finally pots and pans).
- Always use a soft cloth or sponge—**never** use scouring pads or steel wool on dishes.

Storing fine china

- Use a soft pad between plates to separate pieces and prevent scratching. Great padding materials include paper plates, newspaper, corrugated cardboard, felt, bubble wrap, and coffee filters.
- Hang cups from cup hooks or stack cups no more than two tall.

great
Glassware

The process of making glass objects is mystical and fascinating. Watching glass artists in their studios is magical. Silica or sand is heated; soda, potash, and lime are sometimes added. Everything is heated to a high temperature and cooled, crystallizing the medium.

The terms used to describe good glassware are reminiscent of the terms used for fine jewels. You want crystal that's clear in color, with a finish that produces a chiming "ding" when thumped lightly with your fingernail and an appealing design that balances well on the table. (Always check the balance of a glass—when you place it on the table, you don't want to be concerned that it will topple over and break.)

Glassware rims can be rolled or cut. Rolled edges are more durable and less expensive. Cut edges can be scissor-cut or cold cut. Scissor cutting, primarily used on handmade items, has a slightly rounded appearance. The cold cut edge, which is extremely delicate, is used in manufactured fine crystal.

Caring for glasses and stemware

- Wash all stemware and all metal-edged glassware by hand.
- Use a rubber sink mat or wash basin to keep the crystal from clanking in the sink. Add a rubber nozzle to your faucet.
- Wash crystal in warm water with mild detergent.
- **Never** use citrus-based dishwashing detergent on glassware, as it will cloud some surfaces.
- Dry thoroughly before putting away.
- Store in cabinets with the rims up to prevent chipping.

Special cases

- To remove stains from inside glass vases, try rinsing with a solution of white vinegar, lemon juice, and uncooked rice. Or use denture cleaning tablets and warm water.
- Chipped wine glasses can be repaired by a qualified restorer.

choosing glassware

TYPE	DESCRIPTION	QUALITY	DURABILITY	+/-
Crystal	Glassware made of lead and glass that is fired at high temperatures. Quality is determined by the method of manufacture (hand or machine), percentage of lead oxide, the intricacy of the design, and the way it is cut. May be slightly less expensive than lead crystal.	Crystal can be mouth-blown, machine-made, or molded. Higher quality crystal is handmade and has a higher percentage of lead oxide. The intricacy of the design and maker's skill also contribute to overall quality.	Depends on the quality and weight of the glass. Very thin crystal is delicate and must be handled with extreme care.	- May be too formal for your lifestyle.
Lead Crystal	Crystal with a minimum of 24% lead oxide. Prized for its brilliance and clarity. Usually mouth-blown; may be hand-cut, etched, or engraved.	Usually identified by its brilliance. Quality is determined by clarity, cut, color, and balance. Best-quality pieces make a chiming "ping" when lightly tapped. Well-made lead crystal is the highest quality glassware available.	Lightweight and durable.	+ Beautiful. - Should be hand washed. - Can be expensive.
Kali Glass	Glass made with potash is known as Kali glass. It is similar to crystal in appearance but not as clear.	Can be of good quality, depending on the manufacturer. Look for glass without obvious debris, bubbles, or lines.	Very durable.	+ Suitable for daily use.
Soda Lime Glass	Used for bottles, window glass, and many contemporary glassware lines. Consists of limestone, sand, and cullet (broken glass and sand).	Quality depends on method of manufacture. Check glassware for clarity, freedom from debris or bubbles, evenness of the finish, and a good balanced design.	Highly durable.	+ Usually dishwasher safe. + An affordable choice for everyday glassware.
Recycled Glass	Made from used jars and bottles that are melted. Can have a slight coloration to the surface; typically has bubbles and imperfections that add to its unique character.	Usually a heavier weight; well suited for daily use. Informal. A good choice for the visually adventurous.	Highly durable.	+ Usually dishwasher safe. + Tints in color enhance your table and add individuality. + Imperfections, bubbles, and color (things you avoid in fine crystal) enhance these pieces.

identifying Glassware

Choosing the right glass for the drink can become an obsession—one that sometimes gets out of hand. But a particular glass can make a difference in how things taste. Some glasses—primarily fine and handmade wine glasses—allow the liquid to hit your tongue in just the right spot for maximum enjoyment. All glasses make a difference in how things look.

When you are assembling glassware for your cupboards, consider acquiring a complete set, which consists of stemmed water glass, red wine glass, white wine glass, a small tumbler or juice glass, and a large tumbler or highball. (You may, of course, add all manner of other glasses and be the envy of your glassware-conscious neighbors.)

Here is a chart to help you choose shapes for your cabinet:

red wine Red and full-bodied wines need to breathe and benefit from the globe-shaped bowl.

white wine The slimmer bowl shape is designed for younger wines and those that don't need to breathe.

water goblet This oversized globe is used to serve water with the meal.

champagne flute — Tall, elegantly shaped stems slow the escape of bubbles and encourage the effervescent quality of champagnes and sparkling wines.

champagne glass — This saucer-shaped bowl is a less desirable but acceptable way to serve champagne.

martini glass — Of James Bond fame, this stemmed glass can hold any cold cocktail or sherbet.

margarita glass — The wide rim is just right for dipping in salt.

grappa glass — This glass is designed to let the drink hit your mouth without the smell hitting your nose.

brandy snifter — This glass in designed so you can sniff your drink as you sip. It fits comfortably in your hand.

double old fashioned — For any alcoholic drink with ice.

highball — For alcoholic drinks that include a mixer, such as tonic or soda, and ice.

pilsner — The shape enhances and controls the head and foam of beer and ale.

juice tumbler — Small glasses for morning fruit juices and small hands.

functional
Flatware

In the early 1800s people ate with a knife and spoon and the fork was considered dangerous and suspicious. Years ago, sterling silver flatware was a prized possession of young brides starting a household. Now, because silver is so expensive, it doesn't see daily use in most homes. Beautiful flatware made from a variety of materials is available at stores in an array of inspiring designs. In many parts of the world, chopsticks—those beautiful and elegant tools—are the accepted table cutlery, and many people eat their soup from china spoons. Flatware on the table adds depth and strength to a place setting. It sets a boundary around the plate and should line up with the bottom rim of the plate. Only cutlery that will be used during the meal is placed on the table.

The types of flatware and the placement of the pieces signal the intent of the meal and tell you the order of what will be served. A spoon to the right of the plate on the outside, for example, announces a soup course will start the meal.

TYPE	DESCRIPTION	QUALITY
Sterling Silver	Cutlery must be stamped with the word "STERLING" to qualify as authentic. These pieces are made of at least 92.5% pure silver and 7.5% of another metal, such as copper. Knife blades are made of stainless steel.	Impressive; heirloom quality. The weight and intricacy of the pattern determine the cost.
Silver Plate	Flatware made of a base metal or alloy such as nickel, copper, or zinc that is electroplated with pure silver.	Measure the quality of this cutlery by the thickness of the silver plating. Heavier and more intricate patterns are the highest quality and price.
Stainless Steel	Cutlery made of chromium, iron, and nickel.	Weight and balance determine the quality. Pieces marked 18/8 and 18/10 (numbers that signal the percentage of chromium and nickel) are the heaviest and highest quality. (The higher the number, the harder the steel.) Unmarked pieces usually are of lighter weight (and lesser quality).
Pewter	Flatware made of an alloy of tin, copper, antimony, bismuth, and (sometimes) lead.	Our forebears used it for everyday tableware; some pieces are quite valuable. It can be used every day, but should be tested first for lead content.
Plastic	Any eating utensil made of plastic.	These are made to be disposable, but can be re-used. Heavier plastic pieces are best. (It's frustrating to break your fork mid-meal.)

caring for silver

- Never let pieces sit in water overnight or soak for long periods of time.
- Rinse after use to remove acids deposited by foods (e.g., citrus juices, eggs, salt).
- Avoid lemon-scented detergents; they may harm the finish.
- Harsh detergents may pit silver; dilute detergent in hot water before washing cutlery.
- Wash stainless steel and sterling silver separately.
- Dry with a soft cloth.

- Polish once or twice a year with a quality paste and a soft cloth. Use a lengthwise rubbing motion to polish. Avoid hard rubbing so as not to scratch or dent.
- Allow silver to cool completely before storing.
- Store in a dry dark place on a padded or soft surface. Do not store loose in a drawer—pieces can become scratched and marred.
- Keep away from harsh sunlight; contact with wood, dampness, aluminum foil, newspaper, and rubber bands; direct prolonged contact with plastic (plastic cutlery trays, plastic wraps).

DURABILITY	USES	+/-
Sterling can get dings and scratches if handled roughly. Proper storage and cleaning allow generations of use.	Sterling used every day develops a beautiful patina. Used for formal occasions or "company" because of its value.	- You can't put it in the dishwasher. - You have to polish it. + Most beautiful of all flatware available.
The silver plate will wear away over time but it can be replated and should last fairly well with proper care.	Everyday use is rewarding because of its beauty. Many people choose silver plate for their "good" flatware because of its relative affordability compared to sterling silver.	- Washing in the dishwasher is not recommended. - You have to polish it from time to time. + Beauty and weight are its positive aspects.
Highly durable and long lasting.	The preferred flatware for everyday use in most of the fork-wielding world. Used in restaurants and homes everywhere.	+ Dishwasher safe and easily maintained. + Sturdy and useful.
A family heirloom if cared for properly. It melts at 450 degrees F. and if exposed to moisture, can develop oxidation that cannot be repaired.	Can be used everyday, but because of the drawbacks, it is used most often for special occasions.	+/- Pewter is usually made in heavier, chunkier designs and has a rustic, primitive appearance. - Cannot be washed in the dishwasher. + Doesn't tarnish like silver. It develops a lovely soft patina over time and sets a handsome table, especially as an accent.
Best quality lasts and can be re-used.	Picnics and outdoor gatherings. Events that include large groups of people.	+/- You can throw it away; it's lightweight. + Can add a bright color accent to the table that you cannot achieve with silverware.

proper Place Settings

These rules will help guide you, but remember a rule can always be broken. Every table can be different. Different occasions call for different kinds of settings. Dinner for the boss may be more formal than the everyday breakfast crush! As table setting traditionally is the duty of the children in the family, you may choose to educate and decorate at the same time.

- Start with an empty table. *That seems simple enough. Tablecloths, placemats, and pieces of paper are used only to protect the table. You may use nothing at all!*

- Allow plenty of elbow room—24" to 30" for each diner. *I expand my dining room table by putting a blanket over the table and laying a large piece of plywood on top. With a pad and a tablecloth to cover the plywood, I can suddenly seat 12!*

- Place the place setting 1" from the edge of the table.

- Line up flatware with the bottom of the charger or plate in the order in which it will be used, working from the outside in. Place only those pieces that will be used.

- Place knives to the right of the plate, with the cutting edge toward the plate. Place a soup spoon for a first course at the right of the plate on the outside of the knives. Place a seafood or cocktail fork to the right of the soup spoon.

- Place the butter spreader diagonally on the bread plate, with the cutting edge toward the forks.

- Place forks to the left of the plate, with a salad fork to the left of the dinner fork. If the salad is to be served following the main course or if the salad fork is to be used for dessert, it should be to the right of the dinner fork.

- The dessert spoon and fork may be placed above the plate, with the spoon handle to the right above the fork with its handle to the left.

Before you start, check your linens, dishes, flatware, and glassware. Clean, wash, and dry everything you plan to use.

Breakfast

1 Breakfast plate
2 Cereal bowl
3 Napkin
4 Fork
5 Knife
6 Cereal spoon
7 Bread and butter plate
8 Water glass
9 Juice tumbler
10 Cup and saucer for tea
   or coffee

Luncheon

1 Luncheon plate
2 Salad plate
3 Napkin
4 Fork
5 Knife
6 Teaspoon
7 Soup spoon
8 Bread and butter plate
9 Water glass
10 Wine glass

Afternoon Tea

1 Dessert plate
2 Napkin
3 Dessert fork (When no
  knife is placed, the fork
  goes to the right of the
  plate.)
4 Teaspoon
5 Teaspoon or demitasse
  spoon
6 Cup and saucer

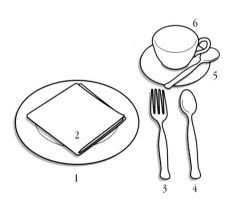

Dinner

1 Plate
2 Napkin
3 Salad plate
4 Fork
5 Knife
6 Teaspoon
7 Bread and butter plate
8 Water goblet
9 Wine glass

Formal Dinner

1 Dinner plate
2 Napkin
3 Fish fork
4 Dinner fork
5 Salad fork
6 Dinner knife
7 Fish knife
8 Soup spoon
9 Bread and butter plate
10 Dessert fork
11 Dessert spoon
12 Water goblet
13 Dessert wine
14 Main course wine
15 Champagne or white wine

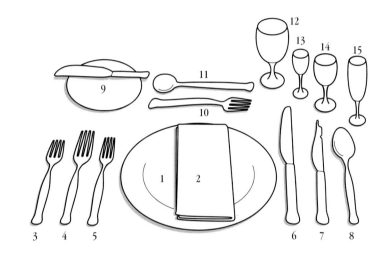

A Buffet

1 Salad
2 Vegetable
3 Bread
4 Meat fork
5 Meat platter
6 Napkins
7 Glasses
8 Flatware

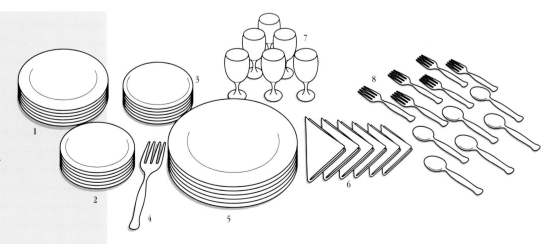

Flowers and Fruit
for focus

Every table is made complete with the addition of a focal point. Traditionally, this focal point is the centerpiece and is placed in the **center** of the table (thus the name), but a focal point placed elsewhere can still be called a centerpiece.

Here are my "rules" about centerpieces:
- Keep them low so that you can see your companions and talk if you are all sitting.
- Keep them tall if it is a standing buffet and the centerpiece is behind the food.

- Set the table first so that you can see how much space you will have in the center of the table.
- Take cues for color from your linens and dishes. Either complement the color or contrast with another color for highlight.
- Don't use anything with a heavy scent that will interfere with food (e.g., potpourri, highly scented candles) or that will wilt and molt and get on your plate (e.g., fragile wildflowers, weeds that are overly dry).

Centerpieces that always work

Fresh fruit
Fresh flowers
Floating candles
Dried pods, nuts
Wrapped twigs or vines
Potted plants
Signature china pieces, such as tureens, bowls, or porcelain lids
Fans
Rocks
Baskets of bread
Pitchers

Metric
Conversion Chart

Inches to Millimeters and Centimeters

Inches	MM	CM
1/8	3	.3
1/4	6	.6
3/8	10	1.0
1/2	13	1.3
5/8	16	1.6
3/4	19	1.9
7/8	22	2.2
1	25	2.5
1-1/4	32	3.2
1-1/2	38	3.8
1-3/4	44	4.4
2	51	5.1
3	76	7.6
4	102	10.2
5	127	12.7
6	152	15.2
7	178	17.8
8	203	20.3
9	229	22.9
10	254	25.4
11	279	27.9
12	305	30.5

Yards to Meters

Yards	Meters
1/8	.11
1/4	.23
3/8	.34
1/2	.46
5/8	.57
3/4	.69
7/8	.80
1	.91
2	1.83
3	2.74
4	3.66
5	4.57
6	5.49
7	6.40
8	7.32
9	8.23
10	9.14

INDEX